## FOREWORD

THIS is a book for beginners. Its aim is (a) to provide plenty of easy material, suitably graded, since confidence and fluency in sight-singing can only be developed by success, and (b) to teach by practice the small amount of basic knowledge necessary for reading music.

The ability to sing, stepwise, up and down the tonic-sol-fa scale is almost a pre-requisite. Where it is not present it should be acquired right at the start, the earliest exercises being sung first from a simple modulator and then from a large stave on the blackboard. The singers should always point at the notes as they sing them, and sing first to the tonic-sol-fa syllables and afterwards to vocalised sounds and even to words if the teacher (or class) cares to provide them.

Ultimately indeed, singers should be able to read words and music simultaneously, but it must be emphasised that this is an elementary book, and one which it is hoped the class will be able to manage right to the end. So often as sight-singing books get harder, the class ceases to be able to "read" the exercises and either the book is abandoned or else the class laboriously "learns" the exercises, which is a waste of time.

After the earliest exercises the material is largely the simple hymn tune (in ordinary time values) or folk tune. Plenty of further material can therefore be found in the hymn-book and song-book, but it must be chosen carefully. *The Folk Song Sight Singing Series* (O.U.P.) has been freely drawn upon, but with a different principle of grading from that followed there. Here stepwise practice and the open key come first. The scheme of this book had its origins in *Eyes Right* by Cyril Winn, to whom grateful acknowledgement is made.

The number of exercises attempted in any lesson must be governed by the ability of the class. Sight-singing should obviously occupy no more than part of a singing lesson and when that time has been spent it is unwise to continue in the hope of "getting on". However much or little has been achieved in that time, the class should always be left with a feeling of confidence. To this end it is often a sound principle to include some earlier easier exercises as revision.

To help in finding *doh* it is as well to point out very frequently that the last sharp in the key signature is *te* and the last flat *fah*, but it is not enough merely to remind the class of this principle—it must constantly be practised if recognition is to be instantaneous.

*B. W. A.*

T0056060

# SING AT SIGHT

by

WILLIAM APPLEBY

*Learn:* When there are no SHARPS (♯) or FLATS (♭) **DOH** is either 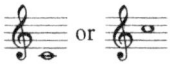 or 

*Learn:* When the bottom figure of the time signature is 4 (as here 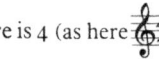 ) ♩ (CROTCHET) is one beat long.

*Learn:* When the notes go **UP**, you go **UP**, and when the notes go **DOWN**, you go **DOWN**.

*Sing:*

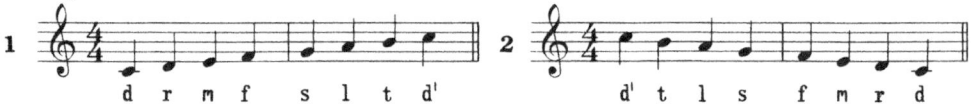


*Learn:* When ♩ (crotchet) is one beat long, 𝅗𝅥 (MINIM) is two beats long.

*Sing:*

*Learn:* When ♩ (crotchet) = 1, 𝄽 (crotchet rest) = 1 beat rest.

*Sing:*

© Oxford University Press 1960 Printed in Great Britain
OXFORD UNIVERSITY PRESS, MUSIC DEPARTMENT, GREAT CLARENDON STREET, OXFORD OX2 6DP
Photocopying this copyright material is ILLEGAL.

*Learn:* When the notes stay still, *you* stay still.
*Sing:*

*Learn:* When there is one sharp (♯) doh is  or 
*Sing:*

*Learn:* When there is one flat (♭) doh is either  or 

*Sing:*

*Learn:* A DOT after a note makes it half as long again. Thus if 𝅗𝅥 (minim) = 2, then 𝅗𝅥. (dotted minim) = 3.

*Sing:*

46
47
48
49
50
Learn:
d m s d' s m d
Sing:
51
52
53
54
55
56

57
58
59
60
Learn:
s, d m s m d s,
Sing:
Tune: Richmond
61
Tune: Hanover (Croft)
62
Learn: Passages between dots (like the four bars below) must be repeated. D.C. al Fine means go back to the beginning and continue to the word FINE (finish).
Sing:
Welsh
63
FINE
D.C. al Fine
Try to sing the PHRASES (marked ⌒) in one breath.
German (adapted)
64
FINE
D.C. al Fine
Learn:
m s d' s m s d
Sing:
French
65

*Learn:* When ♩ (crotchet) = 1, 𝅝 (SEMIBREVE) = 4.

*Learn:*

*Learn:* When there are two sharps, doh is either  or 

*Learn:*

*Learn:* When 𝅗𝅥 (minim) = 2, 𝄼 (minim rest) is 2 beats rest.

*Learn:* When there are two flats doh is either  or 

*Learn:*

*Sing:*

**78** German

*FINE* *D.C. al Fine*

*Learn:*
> means accent the note.
⌒ joining the same notes means keep on. This mark is called a TIE.

*Sing:*

**79** German

**80** British

**81** Hungarian (adapted)

*Learn:* **c** as a time signature is the same as $\frac{4}{4}$

*Sing:*

**82** Danish

French (shortened)
83
FINE
D.C. al Fine
Learn: When there are 3 sharps doh is
and 4 flats
Sing:
French
84
Tallis' Canon
85
Tune: Stuttgart
86
French
87
Tune: Haslemere
88
German
89
Dutch
90

Piae Cantiones
91
German
92
Learn: When there are three flats doh is either
or
and four sharps
or
Sing:
Tune: Benvenuto (Webb) (slightly adapted)
93
German
94

British
95
British
96
Tune: Franconia
97
Tune: St. Peter (Reinagle)
98
Hungarian
99
Polish
100

*Learn:* Halve a crotchet (♩) and you get a QUAVER (♪). Quavers are often joined together like this ♫

*Sing:*

*Learn:* The dot and the jerk ♩. ♪

French
111
Tune: Neander
112
Tune: Rodmell
113
Tune: Samson (from Handel)
114
Tune: Mainz
115
Tune: Moscow
116
Source unknown
117

*Learn:* A sharp in front of a note raises it half a tone like this:

and like this

and this

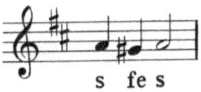


and this

and this

A NATURAL (♮) when it is in front of a flat note does the same thing.

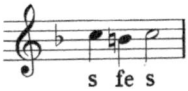

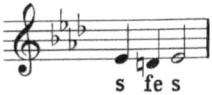


*Sing:*

*Tune:* Melcombe *(Webb)*

118

*Tune:* Llanfair *(R. Williams)*

119

*Tune:* York

120

*Tune:* Capetown

121

*Tune:* Winchester New

122

*Tune:* Dundee

123

Learn: FE often follows ME
m f fe s
m fe s
m f fe s
m fe s
m f fe s
m fe s
etc.
Sing:
124
German
125
B. Helder
126
Tune: Merton (Monk)
127
Tune: Savannah
128
Tune: St. Magnus (J. Clarke)

*Learn:* All the tunes to this point have centred on doh. Most of them have ended on it and many have begun on it. The next group centre on **LAH**, often beginning and ending on it. Tunes centred on doh are called MAJOR tunes; those centred on lah are called MINOR tunes.

We give the tunes names from their central note: a tune centred on C as doh is in C major, but centred on C as lah is C minor.

Some tunes, beginning and ending in the minor, MODULATE (or change) to the major in the middle.

*Learn:* Very often in minor tunes we come across the note **SE** (pronounced "see" or "zee"). It is half a tone higher than **SOH** and is therefore shewn by a sharp or natural. e.g.

*Learn:* Some tunes begin and end in the major, but modulate to the minor in the middle. This usually involves the note **DE**, half a tone higher than doh.

It is sometimes easier to change the whole phrase into the minor:

*Learn:* **TE** made half a tone lower becomes **TA**

In all the tunes up to this point, a crotchet has been worth one beat; and the lower figure of the time signature has been **4**.

In the next fifteen tunes, minims and quavers will also be used as units, and their worth one beat. When a minim is worth one beat,the lower figure will be **2**, and when a quaver is worth one beat, the lower figure will be **8**.

You will also meet the quaver rest (7) SEMIQUAVERS and their rests, the figure and the PAUSE

Also *ff f mf mp p pp*
LOUD - - - - - - - - - - SOFT

Get louder *cresc.* | get softer *dim.* | get slower *rall.*

Sing:
Dutch
146
mf
pp
cresc.
mp
cresc.
mf
British
147
p
mf
p
Welsh
148
mf
cresc.
mf
f
German
149
mf
Thomas Tallis
150

Tune: Vulpius
151
f
dim.
p
When the time signature is 6/8 try to get the feel of 2 beats (each ♩.) in a bar.
British
152
p
cresc.
mf
dim.
p
British
153
p
dim.
pp
get a good jerk and a nice swing
British
154
mf
p
cresc.
mf
French
155
p
cresc.
f
1
2
2nd time dim.
p

Processed and printed by
Halstan & Co. Ltd., Amersham, Bucks., England

OXFORD UNIVERSITY PRESS